Dinosaurs
Had Spikes

KINGFISHER
NEW YORK

Copyright © Kingfisher 2012
Published in the United States by Kingfisher,
175 Fifth Ave., New York, NY 10010
Kingfisher is an imprint of Macmillan Children's Books, London.
All rights reserved.

Written and designed by Dynamo Ltd.

Distributed in the U.S. and Canada by Macmillan,
175 Fifth Ave., New York, NY 10010

Library of Congress Cataloging-in-Publication data has been applied for.

ISBN 978-0-7534-7001-5

Kingfisher books are available for special promotions and premiums. For details contact:
Special Markets Department, Macmillan, 175 Fifth Ave., New York, NY 10010.

For more information, please visit www.kingfisherbooks.com

Printed in China
9 8 7 6 5 4 3 2 1
1TR/0612/HH/-/140MA

Contents

When did dinosaurs live?

The first dinosaurs appeared on Earth about 230 million years ago. The last ones died out roughly 65 million years ago.

Dinosaurs lived on Earth many millions of years, before any people appeared.

All about dinosaurs

- Dinosaurs were a type of animal called a reptile.
- They lived on land, not in the sea or the sky.
- Dinosaur babies hatched from eggs.

Dinosaurs
came in all
shapes and
sizes

5

What did dinosaurs eat?

Some dinosaurs were fierce meat eaters that hunted and killed other animals, but some dinosaurs ate only plants.

Psittacosaurus (sit-**a**-coe-**sore**-us) was a plant eater. It had a tough beak for biting through plant stalks.

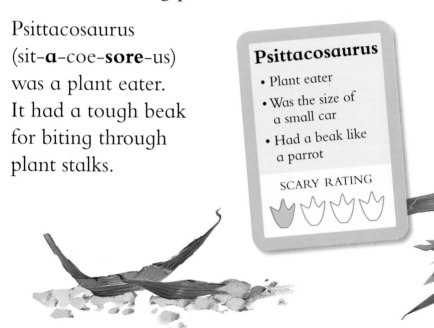

Psittacosaurus

- Plant eater
- Was the size of a small car
- Had a beak like a parrot

SCARY RATING

Psittacosaurus

7

Why did Tyrannosaurus rex have big teeth?

Tyrannosaurus (tie-**ran**-oh-**sore**-us) rex was a scary meat eater. It used its big, sharp teeth to kill other dinosaurs.

A Tyrannosaurus tooth was as long as a banana. It had sharp edges for tearing up food.

Tyrannosaurus rex

- Meat eater
- Was as long as a bus and as tall as an elephant
- Walked on two legs

SCARY RATING

Tyrannosaurus rex

9

Who was bigger than a building?

Some plant-eating dinosaurs were even taller than a modern four-story apartment building. These giants had long necks for reaching up to the tops of trees.

Diplodocus

One of the biggest dinosaurs was called Brachiosaurus (**brack**-ee-oh-**sore**-us).

Brachiosaurus

- Plant eater
- Was as tall as three elephants and longer than two buses
- Had a long neck like a giraffe.

SCARY RATING

Brachiosaurus

Apatosaurus

11

Which dinosaur used its horns for fighting?

Sometimes plant eaters had to fight off hungry meat-eating dinosaurs.

The plant-eating Triceratops (try-**ser**-a-tops) had three sharp horns to frighten its enemies.

Triceratops

- Plant eater
- Was as long as a bus
- Had a bony frill around its head to help protect it

SCARY RATING

Tyrannosaurus rex

Triceratops

13

Why did some dinosaurs have spikes?

Some dinosaurs had spikes to help them fight other dinosaurs.

Stegosaurus (**steg**-oh-**sore**-us) had big spikes on the end of its tail.

Stegosaurus

- Plant eater
- Was the size of a bus
- Had spikes as long as a human arm

SCARY RATING

Stegosaurus

Who had a crest on its head?

Corythosaurus (cor-ith-oh-**sore**-us) had a crest on the top of its head.

It might have been able to blow air through the crest to make a loud, booming noise.

Corythosaurus

- Plant eater
- Was as long as a bus and as tall as a camel
- Head crest might have been colorful, but nobody knows for sure.

SCARY RATING

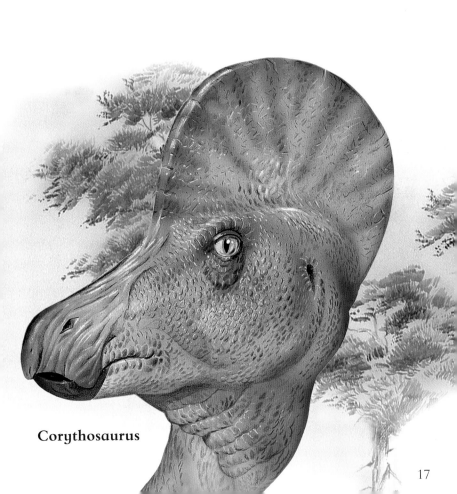

Corythosaurus

Which dinosaur took care of its babies?

A dinosaur called Maiasaura (**my**-ah-**sor**-ah) laid eggs in a nest that it made on the ground.

When the babies hatched, their mother stayed close by to take care of them.

Maiasaura

- Plant eater
- Newborn babies were about 12 in. (30cm) long, roughly as long as a shoebox
- Full-grown Maiasaura were about as long as a bus

SCARY RATING

18

Maiasaura

19

What happened to the dinosaurs?

Nobody knows for sure why the dinosaurs died out. One idea is that giant rocks called meteors crashed into Earth.

The meteors might have thrown up so much dust that the weather on Earth changed and the plants died. Then most of the dinosaurs would have starved.

Remains of the dinosaurs

- Some dinosaur bodies have turned into fossils underground.
- A fossil is a body that has hardened into stone over millions of years.
- Scientists dig up fossils and carefully put the pieces back together—like a jigsaw puzzle.

Meteors falling
from space

23

What do you know about dinosaurs?

You can find all of the answers to these questions in this book.

Did dinosaur babies hatch from eggs?

Were all dinosaurs the same size?

Do dinosaurs still live on Earth today?

What did Tyrannosaurus rex eat?

What did Brachiosaurus eat?

Did dinosaurs live on land or in the sea?

Which is your favorite dinosaur?

23

Some dinosaur words

Beak Hard mouthparts found on birds and some dinosaurs.

Crest A fan-shape that stuck up from the heads of some dinosaurs.

Fossil Part of an animal or a plant that has turned to stone over millions of years.

Frill A bony collar that stuck up around the neck of some dinosaurs.

Horn A hard spike that stuck out of the head of some dinosaurs.

Hunt To catch other creatures to eat.

Reptile A type of animal, such as a snake. Dinosaurs were reptiles.